Sports Illustrated Kids: Legend vs. Legend

SUE BIRD
VS.
CANDACE PARKER

BASKETBALL LEGENDS FACE OFF

by Brendan Flynn

CAPSTONE PRESS
a capstone imprint

Published by Capstone Press, an imprint of Capstone
1710 Roe Crest Drive, North Mankato, Minnesota 56003
capstonepub.com

Copyright © 2025 by Capstone. All rights reserved. No part of this publication may be reproduced in whole or in part, or stored in a retrieval system, or transmitted in any form or by any means, electronic, mechanical, photocopying, recording, or otherwise, without written permission of the publisher.

SPORTS ILLUSTRATED KIDS is a trademark of ABG-SI LLC. Used with permission.

Library of Congress Cataloging-in-Publication Data
Names: Flynn, Brendan, author.
Title: Sue Bird vs. Candace Parker : basketball legends face off / by Brendan Flynn. Other titles: Sue Bird versus Candace Parker
Description: North Mankato, MN : Capstone Press, [2025] | Series: Sports illustrated kids. Legend vs. legend | Includes bibliographical references and index. | Audience: Ages 9–11 Audience: Grades 4–6 | Summary: "Sue Bird and Candace Parker are basketball superstars! Between the two, Bird has more career points, but Parker has more points per game. So which one is the all-time best? Young readers can decide for themselves by comparing the fantastic feats and stunning stats of two legendary pro basketball players"—Provided by publisher.
Identifiers: LCCN 2024020878 (print) | LCCN 2024020879 (ebook) | ISBN 9781669089414 (hardcover) | ISBN 9781669089490 (paperback) | ISBN 9781669089452 (pdf) | ISBN 9781669089513 (kindle edition) | ISBN 9781669089506 (epub)
Subjects: LCSH: Bird, Sue—Juvenile literature. | Parker, Candace, 1986– —Juvenile literature. Women basketball players—United States—Statistics—Juvenile literature. | Women basketball players—United States—Biography—Juvenile literature.
Classification: LCC GV884.B572 F59 2025 (print) | LCC GV884.B572 (ebook) | DDC 796.323092 [B]—dc23/eng/20240515z
LC record available at https://lccn.loc.gov/2024020878
LC ebook record available at https://lccn.loc.gov/2024020879

Editorial Credits
Editor: Ericka Smith; Designer: Tracy Davies; Media Researcher: Svetlana Zhurkin; Production Specialist: Whitney Schaefer

Image Credits
Associated Press: Chris O'Meara, 13, Ted S. Warren, 15; Getty Images: © 2016 NBAE/David Sherman, 21, 27, © 2018 NBAE/Gary Dineen, 9, © 2020 NBAE/Stephen Gosling, 10, © 2022 NBAE/Kate Frese, 11, Andy Lyon, 17, Christian Petersen, 4, 25, 28, Ethan Miller, 6, 8, Gregory Shamus, 16, 19, Jeff Gross, 18, Jonathan Bachman, 23, Jonathan Daniel, 5, Jonathan Moore, 29, Julio Aguilar, 20, Michael Reaves, cover (right), 24, Stacy Revere, 22, Steph Chambers, cover (left), 7, 12, 14, 26; Shutterstock: saicle (background), cover and throughout

Any additional websites and resources referenced in this book are not maintained, authorized, or sponsored by Capstone. All product and company names are trademarks™ or registered® trademarks of their respective holders.

Printed and bound in China. PO 6098

CONTENTS

Basketball Legends Face Off! 4
Scoring 6
Assists 8
Rebounding 10
Steals 12
Blocked Shots 14
College Careers 16
Olympics 18
WNBA Championships 20
All-Star Games 22
Playoffs 24
Awards 26
Who Is the Best? 28

    Glossary 30
    Read More 31
    Internet Sites 31
    Index 32
    About the Author 32

*** All stats current through the 2023 season. ***
Words in **bold** appear in the glossary.

Basketball Legends Face Off!

Sue Bird and Candace Parker were stars of the Women's National Basketball Association (WNBA). Both were first picks in the league's draft. Bird was a small, quick point guard. Parker was a tall, powerful forward.

But who's the best on the court? Let's see how they compare!

Sue Bird

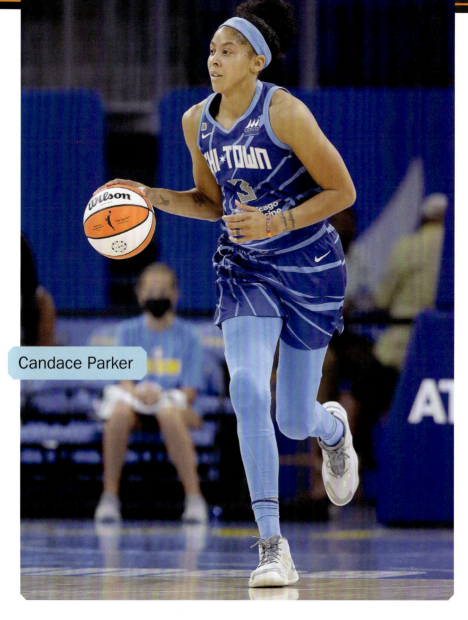

Candace Parker

THE MATCHUP	Height	Weight
Bird	5 feet, 9 inches (175 centimeters)	150 pounds (68 kilograms)
Parker	6 feet, 4 inches (193 cm)	184 pounds (83.5 kg)

Scoring

Parker retired after the 2023 season with 6,574 **career** points. She averaged 16 points a game. Bird retired in 2022 with 6,803 career points. She averaged 11.7 points per game.

Bird ranks second in league history for **three-pointers**. She has 1,001 career three-pointers. Parker only has 342 three-pointers.

Parker shooting a three-pointer in a 2023 game

Bird shooting a three-pointer near the end of her last regular-season game in 2022

THE MATCHUP	Career Points	Points per Game	Career Three-Pointers
Parker	6,574	16	342
Bird	6,803	11.7	1,001

Assists

Point guards rack up a lot of **assists**. Bird's 3,234 assists is the most in WNBA history. Parker was good at setting up teammates for a shot too. She had 1,634 assists.

Bird throwing the ball past Jackie Young of the Las Vegas Aces to her teammate

Parker making a pass for the Los Angeles Sparks

THE MATCHUP	Career Assists
Bird	3,234
Parker	1,634

Rebounding

Parker was one of the best rebounders ever. Her height and long arms helped her snatch up balls as they bounced off the rim. She ended her career with 3,467 **rebounds**. She averaged 8.5 rebounds a game.

Point guards don't usually get many rebounds. Bird had only 1,466 rebounds. She averaged 2.5 rebounds per game.

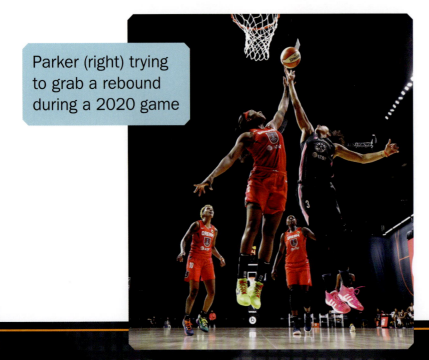

Parker (right) trying to grab a rebound during a 2020 game

Bird rebounding the ball during a game in 2022

THE MATCHUP	Career Rebounds	Rebounds per Game
Parker	3,467	8.5
Bird	1,466	2.5

Steals

Bird used her quick hands to slap the ball away from her opponents. Parker's long arms helped her tip balls to her teammates. Both were quick enough to steal a pass. Bird's 724 career steals rank third of all time. Parker has just 521 steals. But they averaged about the same number of steals per game.

Bird stealing the ball in a 2022 game against the Las Vegas Aces

Parker stealing the ball from a New York Liberty player in 2020

THE MATCHUP	Career Steals	Steals per Game
Bird	724	1.2
Parker	521	1.3

13

Blocked Shots

Parker's height made her a great shot blocker. Her 619 career blocks are fifth on the WNBA all-time list. Bird retired with just 72 blocks.

Parker blocking a shot in 2023

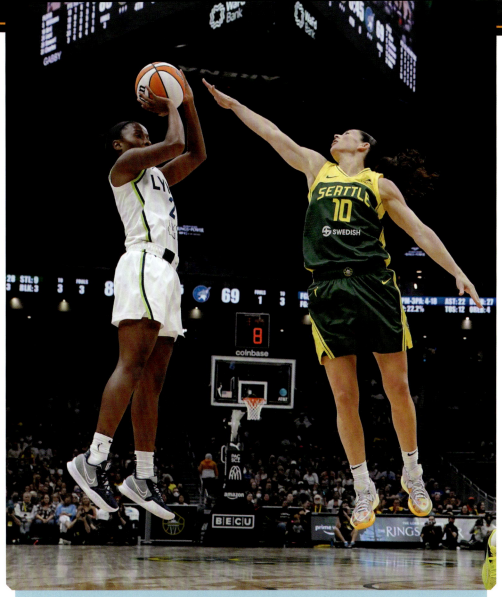

Bird trying to block a shot by a Minnesota Lynx player in 2022

THE MATCHUP	Career Blocked Shots
Parker	619
Bird	72

College Careers

Parker played three seasons at the University of Tennessee. She won two national titles. She was the 2008 Naismith Women's College Player of the Year.

Bird spent four years at the University of Connecticut. She won two national titles too. She was the Naismith Women's College Player of the Year in 2002.

Parker playing in the 2007 NCAA Women's Basketball Championship

Bird competing in a 2002 NCAA Women's Final Four game

THE MATCHUP	College	Years	National Titles	National Player of the Year Awards
Parker	University of Tennessee	2005-08	2	1
Bird	University of Connecticut	1998-2002	2	1

Olympics

The United States has dominated women's basketball in the Olympics. Parker played for Team USA in 2008 and 2012. Bird was on the U.S. squad from 2004 to 2020. Team USA won gold every time.

Parker, Lisa Leslie, and Delisha Milton-Jones celebrating their gold-medal win during the 2008 Olympics

Bird posing with her gold medal from Team USA's 2020 Olympic win

THE MATCHUP	Olympic Appearances	Olympic Gold Medals
Parker	2	2
Bird	5	5

WNBA Championships

Bird spent her entire career with the Seattle Storm. She led them to the WNBA Finals four times. They won the title every time.

Parker went to the WNBA Finals four times too. She won titles with the Los Angeles Sparks, the Chicago Sky, and the Las Vegas Aces.

Bird playing in the 2020 WNBA Finals

Parker in the 2016 WNBA Finals

THE MATCHUP	WNBA Finals	WNBA Titles
Bird	4	4
Parker	4	3

All-Star Games

Bird and Parker were familiar faces at the WNBA **All-Star Game**. Bird was named to the All-Star team a record 13 times. Parker received seven All-Star nominations. Each player sat out one game.

Bird in the 2022 All-Star Game

Parker playing in the All-Star Game in 2017

THE MATCHUP	All-Star Nominations	All-Star Appearances
Bird	13	12
Parker	7	6

Playoffs

Parker and Bird both played well in the **playoffs**. Parker has the second-most playoff points in the WNBA—1,149 points. Bird leads the league in playoff assists. She has 364 assists. And nobody can top Parker's 610 rebounds in the playoffs. Parker also has 117 blocks and 108 steals. Bird has just 12 blocks and 72 steals.

Parker taking a shot in a 2022 playoff game

Bird shooting a three-pointer in the 2018 WNBA playoffs

THE MATCHUP	Playoff Games	Points	Rebounds	Assists	Blocks	Steals
Parker	66	1,149	610	251	117	108
Bird	60	704	164	364	12	72

25

Awards

Bird was one of the best point guards in the WNBA. But she was never the Most Valuable Player (MVP).

In 2008, Parker was the WNBA MVP *and* Rookie of the Year. She was the league's MVP and the All-Star Game MVP in 2013. And in 2016, she was the WNBA Finals MVP.

Bird playing during her final season in 2022

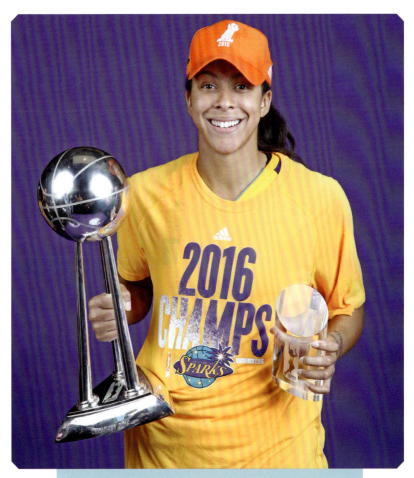

Parker posing with her 2016 WNBA Championship and Finals MVP trophies

THE MATCHUP	WNBA MVP Awards	WNBA Rookie of the Year Award	All-Star Game MVP Awards	Finals MVP Awards
Bird	0	0	0	0
Parker	2	1	1	1

Who Is the Best?

Candace Parker and Sue Bird are among the best to ever play basketball. Bird has the edge in scoring, assists, steals, Olympic gold medals, WNBA titles, and All-Star nominations. But Parker leads in points per game, rebounds, blocked shots, playoff performance, and MVP awards.

Who is the best? You make the call!

Bird shooting a free throw in 2010

Parker taking a shot in 2008

Glossary

All-Star Game (ALL-star GAYM)—a game held every year featuring the best players in the WNBA

assist (uh-SIST)—a pass to a teammate that leads directly to a basket

career (kuh-REER)—including everything between a player's first and last games

playoffs (PLAY-awfs)—the games played after the regular season to determine a champion

rebound (REE-bownd)—a statistic awarded to a player who grabs the ball after a missed shot

three-pointer (THREE POYN-tuhr)—a long shot taken from behind a line on the court that is worth three points

Read More

Flynn, Brendan. *Basketball Records Smashed!* North Mankato, MN: Capstone Press, 2024.

Lowe, Alexander. *G.O.A.T. Basketball Point Guards.* Minneapolis: Lerner Publications, 2023.

Rule, Heather. *Candace Parker.* Lake Elmo, MN: Focus Readers, 2022.

Internet Sites

Naismith Memorial Basketball Hall of Fame
hoophall.com

Sports Illustrated Kids: Basketball
sikids.com/basketball

Women's National Basketball Association
wnba.com

Index

All-Star Games, 22–23, 28
　MVP awards, 26, 27
assists, 8–9, 24, 25, 28
awards, 16, 17, 26–27, 28

blocked shots, 14–15, 24, 25, 28

Chicago Sky, 20
college careers, 16–17

Las Vegas Aces, 8, 12, 20
Leslie, Lisa, 18
Los Angeles Sparks, 9, 20

Milton-Jones, Delisha, 18
Minnesota Lynx, 15

Naismith Women's College Player of the Year, 16, 17
NCAA women's basketball
　championship game, 16
　Final Four, 17

New York Liberty, 13

Olympics, 18–19
　appearances, 18–19
　gold medals, 18–19, 28

playoff performance, 24–25, 28

rebounds, 10–11, 24, 25, 28

scoring, 6–7, 28
Seattle Storm, 20
size, 5
steals, 12–13, 24, 25, 28

Team USA, 18, 19

University of Connecticut, 16, 17
University of Tennessee, 16, 17

WNBA Finals, 20–21
　titles, 20, 21, 28

Young, Jackie, 8

About the Author

Brendan Flynn lives in Minnesota. In addition to writing about sports, Flynn enjoys solving crossword puzzles, trying new recipes in the kitchen, and walking around the beautiful lakes of Minneapolis.